F O O D
CHILDREN ENJOY

Peta Jane Gulliver

Foreword by Cecilia Armelin
Photography by Neil Gulliver
Cover and illustrations by Eliza Kendridge

First Edition June 1992
ISBN 0 948603 06 2
© Peta Jane Gulliver 1992

Published by Cornish Connection
The Coach House, Buckyette Farm, Littlehempston, Totnes, Devon TQ9 6ND

Typeset and printed by Gorsefield Graphics
Roche, St Austell, Cornwall PL26 8HX

PETA JANE GULLIVER has training and experience in the Hotel and catering industry and has also spent some years in residential social work.

During the past nine years she has studied with leading European, American and Japanese teachers of natural healing and Macrobiotic cooking. During the last six years she has been teaching Macrobiotic cooking classes and runs a Macrobiotic Guesthouse. Her interests include organic gardening, permaculture, traditional Celtic Lore and Women's Spirituality. She is also studying and practising crystal healing.

Peta Jane is married to Neil Gulliver who is an Associate Teacher of the Kushi Institute and a Registered Practitioner and teacher with the Shiatsu Society. They have three children: Johnathan, born Easter Sunday 1985; Amanda, born Boxing day 1986; Fredrick, born June 1991.

Together they are creating their family home in Suffolk, "Lifeways", as a place to welcome guests and students who wish to share and learn more about Natural living and Healing within a Macrobiotic context.

Acknowledgements

I wish to thank all the mothers who kindly sent me their childrens favourite recipes: Mary, Lorretta, Heather, Michele, Ann, Kim, Carol, Jay, Wendy, Linda, Montse, Marion, Marion, Dora, Lesley, Barbara, Mary, Alison, Tamara, Salai: without whom this book would not have been possible. I also acknowledge the support of other mothers, who were too busy to put pen to paper, but encouraged me to write this book.

My thanks to Cecelia for writing the foreword for this book.

I also wish to express my heartfelt thanks to everyone who has taught me Macrobiotic cooking during the past several years: Sally Musson, Anna Mackenzie, Susan Stokes, Wieke Nelissen, Geraldine Walker and Aveline Kushi.

Grateful thanks to those who helped compile this book: Neil for his photography and proof reading, Eliza for the beautiful cover picture, and Oliver for kindly publishing.

Contents

Foreword

Cecelia Armelin, B.Sc., Dietitian

This book of easy and delicious recipes for children will give many parents the added confidence and help to provide their families with what I consider ideal nutrition; a way of eating based on Macrobiotic principles. If such practices were widely adopted they would support environmental recovery as well as building the foundation for a population sound in health: physically, mentally and socially. According to my clinical and social experience, the Macrobiotic way of eating urgently deserves recognition as an essential part of true holistic health and healing which may be applied anywhere in the world and particularly among its children.

In 1969 I started working as sole dietitian for a children's hospital in Dublin, Ireland. Over the years I have been struck by the increasing amount of childhood and adult illness that may be cured, healed or prevented by diet. The main foods that have needed to be severely reduced or eliminated are animal meats and fats, milk and dairy produce, refined sugar and unneccessary food additives. Much of my consultation time is spent advising of the joys of eating whole cereal grains, fresh vegetables, legumes and sea vegetables. After discovering Macrobiotics in 1983 I began to re-orientate my own diet and soon noticed personal benefits. In 1986 I began to give dietary advice in wholefood shops and also to see private clients for dietary guidance. Especially since applying Macrobiotics to my work I have witnessed a wide spectrum of illnesses become healed.

What I find most frustrating as a dietician is the lack of interest or co-operation from medical doctors and Government in supporting any clinical studies on the benefits of curative diet for medically diagnosed illnesses; particularly in respect of the increasing number of children with eczema, asthma, arthritis, diabetes, irritable bowl syndrome and intestinal cancer — such as I have been called upon to help. However, while my professional work has been largely of a clinical nature, it has been rewarding to note the positive effects of healthy eating in family life. One does not have to be ill to qualify for the delights of Macrobiotic meals! Children positively enjoy the variety, freshness, tastes and colours of real home cooking as opposed to mechanized convenience fodder. Experience suggests that once children have been lovingly enchanted with healthy eating patterns they will voluntarily maintain this standard in adult life. Living food is a gift of Nature and the birthright of our children.

Cecilia Armelin was Dietitian at a major children's hospital in Dublin from 1969 to 1991, and now works on a freelance basis.
(See address list at the end of this book).

Introduction

Every parent wants the best for their children and, as we now realise, food plays a major part in our health and happiness. We therefore need clear information on what to cook and eat. If you look to the modern media for guidance you will receive many conflicting opinions, and some very obvious false information.

Macrobiotics offers a philosophy on eating and cooking which is based on historically proven practical experience.

In writing this book I wanted to share the experiences of other parents like myself who are bringing up healthy, happy children on meals based on Macrobiotic guidelines.

All the recipes given are the favourite dishes of children, and not a set of recipes that ought to be good for them. As you will see, there is a wide range of food that children really enjoy, and which also meet the criterion of being healthy wholefood. We must be careful not to be too rigid with childrens' diets. If they are healthy and strong, they can process most foods providing you supply whole grains and seasonal vegetables and fruits as the centre of their diet.

It is important not to make children feel socially isolated by their food, and so I have included the names and ages of each child who has contributed to this book, so that your children can see that others also enjoy this food.

The guidelines on weaning foods and balanced meals, while based on Macrobiotic advice, have been tempered with the personal experience of mothers in Great Britain and so are appropriate for our climatic needs and our current experience.

The major ingredient we can add to our cooking is love. The eating of food should be the coming together of the family to joyfully partake in a meal. Yes, I know the temptation is to feed the children separately because of the mess and havoc they can create at the table, and then to allow the adults to eat in peace and quiet. But I sincerely believe that if we want to eat natural wholefoods and create wholeness in our lives and our children's lives then to eat together is a part of that wholeness. From our own experience we have persisted in placing the food on a table and sharing it out on our plates and eating together with our children. The low-level table in our house is 14 inches from the floor so as to include children from the youngest age. The other thing we have always done is to pause before eating, hold hands and chant "Su". This has a remarkably calming effect and helps us harmonize together. (I've even seen the children hold hands and chant together so as to start eating before Neil and I arrive at the table.) I cannot say it has always been easy; as babies they have climbed on to the table, taken too much of some food, spilled food on the floor etc., but they do soon learn what to do and how to behave, and now they are a pleasure to eat with, and can be taken out to eat anywhere.

Recently we have learnt a new chant, and now include it in our pre-meal ritual. We offer this to you to share with your family.

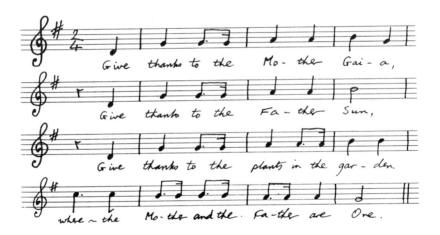

Part I
Childrens' Favourite Meals

Jonathan   *Aged 6*   *from Suffolk*

Amanda   *Aged 4½*

The foundation of Jonathan and Amanda's diet is their breakfast. Each day must start with a bowl (or two) of whole grain porridge, usually of oats and rice mixed, and cooked until very soft. They flavour their porridge with tahini and corn & barley syrup. The porridge is usually served with toasted nori and roasted seeds — pumpkin or sunflower. They also enjoy a lightly seasoned vegetable soup at breakfast.

Some of their other favourite dishes are as follows:

Sweet Daikon Pickles

Thinly slice two cups of daikon, toss it with ½ teaspoon sea salt and let sit 5-8 hours.

Pour off excess water.

Combine 3 tablespoons each of umeboshi vinegar, rice syrup and water in a small saucepan, simmer one minute then allow to cool to room temperature.

Pack the sliced daikon into a jar, pour the liquid mixture over, then cover with a lid and light weight to keep the vegetables submerged.

Allow to sit at room temperature for 1-2 days, then refrigerate.

All pickles are enjoyed by Jonathan and Amanda.

Best shop-bought ones are Eden Mixed Pickles.

Arame Rolls

Filling	**Pastry**
Arame, onion and carrot in equal proportions	*1 cup flour (ww. or 85%)*
	3 tablespoons sesame oil
Shoyu	*¼ -½ cup of water*
Oil	*Pinch of salt*

Filling

Grate carrots, soak arame and slice onions. Saute onions in a little oil for 3-4 minutes — add carrots for a further minute then strain arame (reserve liquid) add and saute also for one minute.
Add the liquid from soaking the arame and a little shoyu. Simmer for 40-50 minutes, the longer the onions and carrots cook the sweeter the filling will taste. Add more shoyu two minutes before the end of the cooking time.

Pastry

Sieve flour and add the salt.
Add oil, rubbing into the flour between the palms of your hands.
Add water and then knead for five minutes.
Put in the fridge for 30 minutes.
Roll out into an oblong 4" wide. Put the filling 1½" wide along the middle of the pastry. Wet one side and then fold over the pastry and fold together.
Prick top of rolls and cut into 1" individual rolls.
Put onto oiled baking tray and bake for 15-20 minutes. Gas mark 6.

Sushi Rolls

Nori sheets	*Cooked brown rice*
Fillings	**Flavourings**
Cabbage strips, blanched	*Sesame spread*
Carrot strips, blanched	*Miso*
Spring onions, blanched	*Mustard*
Daikon, blanched	*Chutneys*
Pumpkin strips, blanched	*Umeboshi*
Smoked mackerel	*Peanut butter*

Toast one side of the nori sheet and then place on a bamboo sushi mat.
Using wet hands cover two thirds of the nori with brown rice about ⅛" thick,
pressed down firmly.
Put a strip of fillings and flavourings on the rice across the width of the sheet.
Carefully roll like a Swiss roll, using the mat to help roll the sushi.
Press firmly together.
Cut 8 equal portions and serve on a plate.

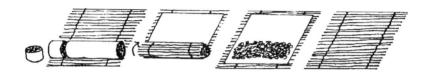

These take a little practice, but once you get the hang of it, are simple to make.
I usually put in carrots and cabbage to get a nice colour contrast, then some
mustard and tahini for taste, and you have a simple but delightful sushi.
Smoked mackerel with vegetables and sesame spread makes a rich sushi for
special occasions.
Use your imagination for variations of vegetables and flavourings.
Alternatively to brown rice you can put in cooked noodles, but this can be a
little more difficult to make,
Sushis are useful to take on picnics.

Creamy Cucumber Soup

2 cucumbers   1 onion

½ cup oat flakes

Sweet miso or salt to taste
Peel and thinly slice onions. Cut cucumbers into ¼" slices — discard ends.
Add to pot with 1½-2 pints water, cucumber, onions and oats.
Bring to boil and simmer for 15 minutes.
Put through a hand mouli or liquidize.
Return to pot and season with sweet miso or salt.
Simmer two minutes longer.
This is Amanda's number one favourite recipe.
It is also good for breast feeding mothers to help with milk.
Keep seasoning very light.

Thick Noodle and Vegetable soup

1 carrot thinly sliced

1 onion or leek thinly sliced

¼ cauliflower into small florets

6" strip of wakame or purple nori soaked and cut up

1 block tofu diced ¼" squares

Watercress

Shoyu to season

1 packet Udon noodles

Bring a large pan of water to boil, while it is coming to the boil cut up all the vegetables.
When the water is boiling add noodles and first four vegetables.
Cook until all ingredients are fairly soft 15-20 minutes. Add tofu and shoyu.
Cook further five minutes. Add watercress and turn off heat.
Serve immediately.
This is a frequent and favourite lunch for my two! The vegetables can be varied and you can use smoked or plain tofu. Also dried tofu in winter — add with the vegetables at the beginning.

Carrot Salad

2 carrots washed   *2 apples peeled*

1 tablespoon umeboshi vinegar

Grate carrot on fine grater and then the apple.
Season with umeboshi vinegar and you have a quick refreshing dish for warm weather.

Parsnip Chips

Cut parsnips into mátchsticks (e.g. cut slices and then cut along length of slice).
Bring deep fried oil up to frying temperature.
Put in parsnip chips and cook until golden and crispy.
Remove and drain chips. Sprinkle with a little salt.
A favourite winter dish.

Carrot Cake

7 oz. sesame oil	*1½ oz. butter (optional)*
7 oz. flour (85% or ww)	*4 oz. corn & barley syrup*
2 finely grated carrots	*1 finely grated apple*
Handful currants (optional)	*2 teaspoons baking powder*
4 tablespoons water	*Oil for tin*

Melt butter and corn & barley syrup in a saucepan until runny. Remove from heat, add oil and mix well. Sift the flour and baking powder into a mixing bowl. Add oil mixture gradually — stirring well.
Add carrots, apple and currants.
If required add water. Should be quite a sloppy mix.
Put in a 6½" cake tin. (One with a push up bottom is easiest). Or in little bun tins.
Pre-heat oven Gas mark 4, 350 F, 180 C.
Cook for 25-30 minutes.
Check with a skewer to see if centre of cake is cooked.

Blackberry & Apple Pie

Pie Crust	Filling	Topping
1 cup flour ww or 85%	*Blackberries*	*Chopped hazel nuts*
3 tablespoons sesame oil	*Apples*	*Corn & barley syrup*
Pinch of salt	*Pinch of salt*	
¼-⅓ cup water	*Water*	

Combine salt and flour, rub in oil. Mix in water until you have a kneading dough. Knead for 5 minutes and then place in a cool place for 20 minutes. Roll out and line a pie dish 8-10".
Peel core and slice the apples, dip into salt water for 10 seconds, wash blackberries. Cover pie with greaseproof paper and put in oven Mark6 for 30 minutes. Dry roast hazel nuts in oven 10-15 minutes. Remove and cool. Rub between hands to remove skins and then chop. Melt some corn & barley syrup with a little water then mix in the nuts.
After half an hour remove the greaseproof paper from pie, add the topping and return to the oven for 5-10 minutes.
Good hot or cold. Jonathan has successfully made this himself.

Kim	*Aged 17*	*From Essex*
Kesinee	*Aged 14*	
Oliver	*Aged 12*	

Kim, our eldest son, is at present taking three 'A' levels. A keen athlete and sportsman, he leads a very full life. His great standbys have always been miso soup and bancha tea. He is also very fond of buckwheat pancakes with a sauce of saute onions and miso. Rice cream is another old favourite.

Kesinee loves animals of all kinds. She is a very competent artist and has exhibited and sold her drawings. She also practices Aikido with Kim. Spaghetti has always been her favourite dish with any kind of sauce! She also loves seitan. Cous cous cake with a fruity kuzu sauce is her first choice of sweet.

Oliver has been macrobiotic all his life and is extremely strong and well on it. When he was 10 he lifted 400 lbs. in a straight shoulder lift and is still a very keen rugby player. Like Kim he likes bancha tea and miso soup made with nori and carrots. As a main course, rice, parsnip fritters, cabbage and carrots are his choice, and for dessert our adaptation of a Malay dish called Pulot.

Buckwheat Pancakes

2 cups buckwheat flour	*1 free range egg — beaten*
Pinch of salt	*Corn or sesame oil for frying*
3 cups water	

Mix all ingredients except oil. Heat frying pan, brush lightly with oil, and reduce heat to medium low. Ladle in just enough batter to cover surface of pan. Fry until set. Using a thin spatula, carefully turn pancake to fry the other side.

FILLING: saute onions until soft. Add miso to season.

Seitan

3½ lbs whole wheat flour (or ½ & ½ w.w. and unbleached white)

8-9 cups water

Place flour in a large pot. Add enough warm water (8-9) cups to make it the consistency of bread dough. Knead for 3-5 minutes or until the flour is thoroughly mixed with water. (Kneading can be for longer, but usually mothers are short on time). Cover with warm water and let sit for 5-10 minutes. (This is the minimum soaking time. The dough can stay in the water longer.) Knead again in the soaking water for about 1 minute. The water will turn cloudy or milky.

Place sticky gluten into a large strainer and put the strainer into a large pot or bowl. Stand in sink. Pour cold water over the gluten and knead in the strainer. Repeat until the bran and starch are washed out. Alternate between warm and cold water when you are rinsing and kneading the gluten. This alternating water temperature makes washing out the bran easier. The first and last rinses should always be with cold water to contract the gluten into a large ball.

After you have rinsed and kneaded the bran and starch out of the gluten, wash it again in a bowl for 2-3 minutes with cold water to remove any remaining bran. The gluten should form a sticky ball. Separate the gluten into 5-6 pieces and form balls. drop balls into 6 cups of boiling water, and boil for 5 minutes or until the balls float to the top. Remove and cut into cubes for soup or into strips if you plan to saute it with vegetables. If you intend to make stuffed cabbage rolls or sandwiches with the seitan, leave the cooked pieces whole. Place one 3 inch strip of kombu in the boiling water and add ¼ -⅓ cup of tamari. Place cubed, sliced or whole pieces of gluten into the tamari water. Bring to the boil. Reduce flame to low, cover pot, and simmer for 35-45 minutes.

Kesinee likes her cooked seitan rolled in sesame seeds and deep fried.

Parsnip Fritter

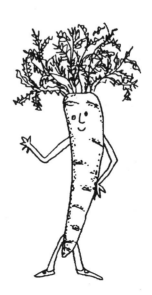

Cooked rice

Grated parsnip

Oil for frying

1-2 pinches salt

Flour and water to bind

Mix and shape into burger shape. Deep fry until golden.

Scott   Aged 14   From Essex

Samuel   Aged 9

Motchi Burgers

   3 cups sweet brown rice   3¼ cups water

   1 pinch salt   Sesame oil for frying

Put sweet rice, water and salt into a pressure cooker and bring up to pressure. Cook for 40-45 minutes. When cooked take a smooth ended rolling pin and pound the sweet rice until very sticky and the grains are broken. This usually requires the help of the boys as it takes some time. It also helps to have the end of the rolling pin wet.

Take approximately 1 tablespoon of motchi and roll into rounds, then flatten into burger shapes and fry in hot sesame oil until golden brown both sides.

Smoked Tofu Fries

   1 packet smoked tofu   2 sheets nori

   ⅔ cup gram (chick pea) flour   ⅔ cup w.w. flour

   Water   Pan of oil (sunflower) to deep fry

Mix the flours with water to make a coating batter.

Leave to stand. Place the two sheets of nori together and cook over gas flame. Cut into ¾ inch wide strips. Cut up tofu into ¼ inch slices approximately 2 inches wide and wrap them with the strips of nori. Use a little drop of water to get the nori to stick. Dip into the batter and put into hot oil. They should sink and then raise to the surface within 1 minute.

Semolina Dessert

   2 cups whole wheat semolina   ⅔ cup ground almonds

   4 tablespoons corn & barley malt Pinch salt

   3 cups water

Place semolina and ground almonds in a cast iron pan and dry roast until you smell the nice aroma — stirring continually with a spatula. (Don't burn).

Put all ingredients in a saucepan and cook for 30 minutes. Place a flame spreader under the pan while cooking.

Serve with some jam (optional) and roasted almonds to garnish. This makes a good fruit free dessert which Samuel enjoys.

Tofu Ice Cream

 4 oz. (125g.) tofu   *½ pint (250ml.) apple juice*

 Sweetener (rice syrup) if needed

Put ingredients in blender and liquidise.
Freeze in a shallow tray until the mixture is slushy.
Liquidise again and re-freeze. Repeat this process to obtain a smooth consistency.
Remove from freezer 10 minutes before serving.
In winter time my children will eat all kinds of stews so long as there are dumplings in it. On the side of the vegetable suet packet is a very quick and easy recipe.
Scott, aged 14, has always eaten well, but has just started being very picky with good food.

Samuel, aged 9, eats very well but craves for sweet things, and given the opportunity will take them behind my back.

Izzy   *Aged 7*   *From Cornwall*
Eldon   *Aged 4*

Seitan Rolls

Prepare uncooked seitan (recipe page 10)

 2 carrots cut into matchsticks   *Barley miso*

 Shoyu   *Fresh ginger 3-4 slices*

 6" strip kombu

Take the prepared seitan and divide up into balls. Wrap each ball around some matchstick carrots with a dab of barley miso.

Bring pan of water to the boil. Put seitan rolls into the boiling water and cook for 5 minutes. Add kombu, ginger and shoyu to strong soup flavour. Simmer for 45 minutes.

Seitan is always eaten within 1 or 2 meals quick as a flash. Always accompanied by a surprising amount of gratitude.

Hijiki & Carrots

Hijiki	*Carrots or squares of white cabbage*
1 tablespoon sesame oil	*Shoyu sauce*

Garnish:

Sesame seeds, roasted almonds or watercress.

Soak the hijiki, cut carrots into slices. When the hijiki is soft strain and cut up. (The soaking water is good for plants.) Saute the carrots and hijiki in oil for 5 minutes, then add a little water to cook for 30 minutes with lid on. Add a little shoyu to season. Put in serving dish, and garnish with roasted sesame seeds or almonds and a sprig of watercress.

This disappears as quickly as the seitan.

Sandwiches

Whole meal pitta bread (steamed or grilled)

or Hovis whole meal sugar free bread

or bread with sunflower & poppy seeds in it

Filling:

Sesame spread (tahine)	*Miso*
Water	*Cucumber or carrot*
Shoyu	*Eden pickles*

Mix two spoonfuls of sesame spread to one of miso creamed with the same amount of water. Spread on bread. Finely cut rounds of cucumber, marinade for about 5 minutes in a few drops of shoyu, or instead of the cucumber Eldon loves grated carrot.

For sandwiches to be acceptable as food they all have to be cut in triangles.

They love to eat Eden pickles after their bread, which helps them to digest it.

Bean Soup

2 cups cooked aduki beans (or use green, brown or red lentils)

3-4 carrots   *4 cups water*

Watercress   *Shoyu or miso to season*

Slice up carrots. Bring water to boil with beans, add the carrots. Cook for 10 minutes then add the watercress and seasoning. Cook 2 minutes more. Mouli in a hand mouli. The children love the creaminess of this soup and prefer it to a plain bean dish.

Ginger Bread Queens

3 cups of dove strong white flour   *1 cup safflower oil*

2 teaspoon cinnamon powder   *1 teaspoon fresh ginger juice*

1 or 2 pinches sea salt   *1 egg*

Water to mix to dough consistency Raisins

Ginger bread queen shaper to cut shapes

Mix first six ingredients together, then add water until it is a dough consistency. Roll out and cut "queens" with the shaper. Use raisins for eyes, crown, buttons, hem of robe etc.

Place ginger bread queens on a well oiled baking tray and cook 20-25 minutes in pre-heated oven reg.4.

We have also used this recipe to make little ginger bread rolls of plaited bread. Izzy loves to do this.

Grilled Fish

Plaice or whole trout   *Shoyu*   *Fresh ginger juice*

Grate 1 inch cube of fresh ginger and squeeze to get the juice.
Slit the fish three times, then place in a marinade of shoyu and the ginger juice for one hour.
Grill gently each side for 6 minutes. Don't let the fish get too hard.
They love this simple fish dish — with eyes in it — served with slices of millet mould or noodles and with steamed carrots and whole green leaves lightly boiled.

The children are happy with a basically macrobiotic diet especially when I explain to them about how good organic, cleanly cooked food is. They love fish fingers and eggs which they have about once a week. When they go to parties they like to eat more widely to experience what other children eat. I try to keep them off junky, chemical foods and over-processed foods and generally they accept that quite happily.

Izzy likes her packed school lunch to conform with other childrens lunch boxes, so has sandwiches, apple juice, little packets of oatcakes, and pieces of fruit — apple or pear or satsuma, sugar free sweets, pop corn etc.

Alexander   Aged 3½   From Buckinghamshire

Alexander enjoys most of his food very simply cooked, like pan- fried tofu, boiled watercress, black olives, clear broth or miso soup without vegetables in. He prefers noodles to rice, and is also attracted to foods like toast and butter, scrambled eggs, yogurt etc.

Here are three simple recipes he will eat.

Garlic Fried Rice

Cooked rice   *Olive oil*   *Garlic clove*

Dice the garlic clove and fry for ½ minute in the olive oil, add rice and cook until it has warmed through.

Red Radish Pickle

Slice red radishes thinly and marinade them in umeboshi vinegar for 1 hour. This makes them a nice pink colour.

Jam Tarts

Pastry:

1 cup flour   *3 tablespoons oil*

¼-½ cup water   *Pinch salt*

Blackcurrant jam.

Mix pastry ingredients to firm dough. Roll out and cut with pastry cutter 4 inch round. Oil bun tins and line with pastry. Put a teaspoon of blackcurrant jam in each tart. Cook for 25-30 minutes.

You can use any jam, but Alexander will only eat blackcurrant, and will not as yet eat other cooked fruits.

| *Joanna* | *Aged 9¾* | *From Norfolk* |
| *Jefferson* | *Aged 5¾* | |

Dumplings

> *1 cup organic white flour*   *1 cup organic brown flour*
>
> *1 cup Broadlands vegetable suet*   *1 pinch salt*
>
> *Water*

Mix dry ingredients together. Add water to make a soft dough. Put in vegetable and bean stew. Cook for 20 minutes.

Favourite vegetables and lentils in a stew are: carrots, peas, onion, cauliflower, green lentils, plus kombu sea vegetable. Seasoned with soya sauce, and thickened with kuzu. Serve with a plate of greens.

Cake

> *5 tablespoons oil*   *2 tablespoons honey*
>
> *½ cup grated fresh coconut*   *½ teaspoon orange or lemon essence*
>
> *10 tablespoons flour — brown or organic white*
>
> *1 teaspoon cream of tartar*   *½ teaspoon bicarbonate*   *Pinch salt*

Mix all ingredients. Oil a baking tin. Add cake mixture.
150°C Put in oven at 300F for 40 minutes. Leave to cool and then eat it.

Joanna's favourite meal is Christmas Dinner which is normally jacket potatoes, pheasant, seitan pie, Yorkshire puddings, Brussels sprouts, roast parsnips and pumpkin, and kale. Her favourite grain is sweetcorn with shoyu sauce and sesame butter.

We grow all our own vegetables and ground our flour for bread, made with cooked sour grain.

Verushka   *Aged 3½*   *From Somerset*

Spaghetti

1 packet wholewheat spaghetti (or any other kind of pasta)

Salt   *2 medium sized onions*

1 clove of garlic (pickled in miso)   *½ tablespoon sesame oil*

Touch of miso   *1 teaspoon kuzu*

Tomato puree   *Parmesan cheese (optional)*

Cook pasta in salted water.

Sauce.

Saute the onions and garlic in oil. When golden add enough water for the quantity of sauce you require. Simmer for about 10 minutes. Add a little tomato puree to add colour and stir. Add kuzu to thicken, and last of all miso. Sprinkle with Parmesan cheese or ground sesame seed.

Rich Fruit Cake

8oz. dates   *10oz. water*

1lb. dried fruit   *6oz. plain 100% flour*

3 teaspoons baking powder   *1 teaspoon mixed spice*

Grated orange rind   *4 tablespoons orange juice*

1oz. ground almonds

Simmer dates in water until soft and mash.
Mix into rest of ingredients.
Put into greased 2lb. tin.

Bake 90 minutes Gas 3, 325F.

160°c

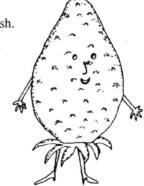

Edward	*Aged 9*	*From Woodstock*
Tim	*Aged 12*	
Robert	*Aged 14*	

I manage to maintain meals without meat, sugar and additives. To include quite a high percentage of more traditional macrobiotic dishes and aim high on organics. However, on many occasions that is where any similarity to a book version of macrobiotics ceases! When I asked for suggestions for the book I was greeted by "fish and chips", "pizza", "steamed marmalade pudding" etc. accompanied by various wicked giggles.

My boys have decided that they do not like things like squash, beans and seaweed, but there are times when I feel they need them 'medicinally', so I have devised ways to 'hide' them or make them more fun. Also the boys have never really liked the Japanese way of cooking, and find it embarrassing when friends call, so much of my cooking is adapted from traditional English fare.

Tim loves to cook and he helped choose these recipes which seem to go down well with his brothers.

Bean (or Tofu) Parcel

8oz. wholewheat flour	*4 tablespoons safflower oil*
Pinch sea salt	*Sufficient water to make a good dough*

2-3 heaped tablespoons kidney, pinto or black eyed beans or
1 block tofu — cut into chunks and deep fried

A variety of sliced seasonal vegetables, sufficient to make about one pint of filling

Cook the beans with a piece of kombu until done. Remove the kombu and mash or chop very finely and return to the beans, so that it will 'disappear' into the mixture.

OR Use the prepared tofu, plus some pre-cooked kombu, wakame or green nori flakes, depending on the energy required. Add the prepared vegetables to the bean mixture, with only just enough liquid to cook.

Add seasoning to your taste towards the end of cooking, using perhaps basil, oregano, thyme, 'Italiano' seasoning or a little organic tomato puree, tamari, teriyaki sauce, or miso (white or barley).

Mix the pastry ingredients together with a wooden form to make a good dough and roll out to approximately 12" square.

Thicken the liquid in the bean/tofu/vegetable mixture slightly with arrowroot or kuzu. (I often find kuzu in a savoury dish too yang for children).

Pour the mixture carefully in the centre of the pastry and fold the corners into the middle, overlapping enough to touch. Secure the corners together with a wooden cocktail stick.

Bake at gas 4 for about 45 minutes. The pastry will slightly shrink and when cooked will show tempting slits of savoury beans and vegetables. Serve with lots of steamed beans or green salad, and sushi ginger. Children love this recipe made with flaky pastry, which may be purchased at a reasonably good quality. I also make it using self raising flour, to make a lighter pastry, especially if we are having visitors.

Children's Favourite Miso Soup

This is made with water or stock, wakame (cooked until very soft, chopped into teeny pieces and used as the 'mystery ingredient'), carrots, onion, red lentils, toasted sunflower seeds, and either barley or white miso. This makes a very sweet soup with interesting textures.

Green Soup

(For children who 'hate' greens)

Stock or water, kombu, a good large quantity of kale/spinach or watercress, onion (chopped small), white miso and a little sea salt, a little soya milk to sweeten.

Cook all the ingredients together for a short time.

(i.e. to keep the greens a lovely fresh green colour).

Remove the kombu and use in another dish. Blend or liquidise the soup until smooth. Kale and spinach make a thicker quality soup, watercress may need a little arrowroot or kuzu to thicken.

Steamed Marmalade Pudding

5oz S.R.Wholewheat flour	*1-2 organic eggs*
4 tablespoons safflower oil	*½ jar of sugar free marmalade*
*2 level tablespoons of honey or maple syrup * *	
1 organic orange	

Oil a 1½pint pudding basin. Slice the top and tail off the whole orange. Slice the remaining orange into 5 slices. Place one slice in the bottom of the basin and the others around the sides. Spoon the marmalade into the bottom of the basin.

Mix the sponge ingredients together and spoon on top of the marmalade, smoothing the top over flat.

Cover with a double oiled piece of greaseproof paper and secure with a piece of string or a large elastic band. Steam in a saucepan for 1½hours.

Turn out of the basin onto a plate to serve on its own, or with soya custard, or a fruit/kuzu sauce.

* This pudding is very good when friends come to tea, but needs to be sweet enough for western children's tastes. Steaming is a good way of eating cooked flour. It could also be used as a steamed jam pudding, or a "Spotted Dick" with dried fruit — omitting the orange.

French Apple Flan

Enough pastry (once again I use S.R. wholewheat flour) to line an oblong dish, approximately 9" X 12".

Core 4 eating apples and slice finely, lengthwise.

Arrange the slices down the pastry in lines.

Glaze with warm sugar free apricot jam or apple juice thickened with kuzu + few grains salt.

Bake regulo 5 for about 30 minutes, or until the apple is soft and the under pastry cooked. Serve warm or cold in slices.

St.Clements Pudding

1 sweet squash	*Piece kombu*	*1 cooking apple*
¾pint apple juice	*The rind and juice of ½-1 lemon*	
Cous cous		

Optional — pinch of salt (depending on children's condition).

Peel the squash and cut into chunks.

Cook the squash in the apple juice, with the kombu, the cored and peeled apple and the lemon rind and juice. When the squash is soft remove the kombu and use for another dish. (The kombu not only adds nutrients and helps balance the acidity of the fruit but also helps the squash to cook).

Add enough cous cous to thicken the mixture to a very soft blancmange consistency, after it has been allowed to swell in the liquid blended or liquidised.
This dessert will thicken considerably as it cools, and is nicest when fairly soft.
Decorate with a little grated lemon rind.

Grape Jelly (Kanten) — Mandarin Jelly (Kanten)

1 bottle or carton of red grape juice
or
1 bottle or carton of mandarin juice and a small tin of sugar free mandarins.

Agar and a few grains of sea salt

Grape Jelly:
Agar does not readily dissolve in red grape juice, therefore dissolve enough agar to set your quantity of juice in a saucepan containing ¾ cup of water, simmering until clear, then quickly add the juice and salt, stirring constantly. Pour into individual glasses and leave to set.

Mandarine Jelly:
Dissolve the agar in the mandarine juice plus the juice from the tin of mandarins and pour into a large shallow dish. Add the mandarine pieces and leave to set.
I find the children hate me using Japanese names when they have friends to tea and so we always use the English equivalent to save them embarrassment. These recipes prove very useful with children who distrust food which does not come out of 'a packet'!

Fried Beans and Taco's

1 pint cooked beans (kidney or pinto), cooked with kombu and reserving the cooking water

1 onion   *1 teaspoon sesame oil*

Basil and oregano to taste   *1 rounded teaspoon barley miso*

Chopped parsley to garnish

Saute the onion in the oil until transparent, then add the beans, kombu, herbs and enough liquid to just cover. Cook until the onion is soft, then add the miso and remove from the heat.
Mash the bean mixture until creamy (a potato masher is good) and test for

flavour. If the beans are too moist to serve with the taco's, then cook a little longer in an open pan until some of the liquid has evaporated — taking care to stir frequently. Serve in warmed taco's or pancakes, garnished with chopped parsley and served with steamed greens and pickles.

Apple and Miso Chutney

10oz cooking apples — peeled and cored

8oz onions — skinned and chopped   *4oz dates — chopped*

2oz dried apricots — chopped or left whole   *2oz raisins*

½ pint organic cider vinegar   *Pinch salt*

¼ teaspoon cinnamon   *¼ teaspoon allspice*

1 level teaspoon barley miso

Cook all ingredients together until the chutney is rich, brown, thick and aromatic. The miso used at the BEGINNING of cooking this chutney helps soften any acidity from the cider vinegar and adds a distinct background mellowness. Children love this in sushi.

Celery/Cucumber/Orange/Dulse Salad

Soak some dulse in a little orange juice. Slice a quantity of celery and/or cucumber and mix with small pieces of fresh orange and a few grains of salt. Check the dulse for shells etc. then chop the dulse finely and add to the salad. Chopped parsley and finely shredded Chinese leaves could also be added. Add a little umeboshi vinegar according to needs.

Aduki Bean Dessert

½ pint cooked aduki beans + kombu

¼ pint cooking water + ¼ apple juice

1 rounded tablespoon raisins Pinch sea salt

1 level tablespoon tahini   Agar

Soak the raisins in the liquid. Cook all the ingredients except the tahini together, using as much agar as you need to create the thickness of dessert which you require for your children's needs. When the agar is dissolved blend or liquidise the aduki mixture with the tahini and serve in individual glasses, decorate with chopped roasted nuts if liked. Non macrobiotic children enjoy this too, but you may feel you need to add a little maple syrup to create a sweeter taste.

The original aduki bean 'fudge' I find far too yang and heavy for children, therefore I have made this into a softer more yin dessert.

When using adukis for children I now always use the original cooking water as a 'medicinal' drink for myself, and add more water for a second cooking for the children. This follows years of experimentation to see how I could get the children to eat them and I can't 'cheat', they instinctively leave them if I do!

Red Dragon Pie

This is similar to 'Shepherd Pie' but made with adukis. Make the bottom layer with adukis cooked with kombu (once more using the second cooking water only for children), plus chopped and sauteed onions, herbs e.g.basil and oregano, carrots sliced into rounds, a little organic tomato puree and seasoned with tamari, miso, teriyaki sauce to taste.

Place this layer in an oven proof dish. Place cooked mashed organic potatoes on the top and score a pattern on the top with a fork.

Bake gas mark 5 for 45 minutes, or until the top is golden brown.

Serve with lots of green vegetables, raw, steamed etc. according to season and condition.

The children have discovered it is good to add some Wholearth 'Tomato' or 'Kensington' sauce to their meal, just as I used to add Heinz tomato sauce to my shepherd pie years ago!

Dearbhail   *Aged 18 months*   *From Dublin*

Rice

   1 cup organic brown rice (short grain) washed

   1 strip kombu or wakame

   9 cups water

Bring to boil and simmer for 4 hours.

Tofu Fingers

1 piece of tofu cut into small fingers. Coat with arrowroot flour and wrap with nori. Shallow fry for 5-10 minutes in sesame oil.

Tempeh Triangles

Cut tempeh into triangles and coat with maize flour and deep fry for 10 minutes.

Stew

Mochi, round fu, carrots, onions, parsnips, dulse.

Saute onions in a little water first, and then add in the rest of the vegetables from yin to yang. Cover with water and bring to the boil and simmer for 15-20 minutes. Can thicken with arrowroot or kuzu if too much water is used.

Yellow Split Pea Stew

Carrots, onions, parsnips, wakame, yellow split peas (washed).

Saute onions first in water, then add rest of vegetables in order from yin to yang. Cover with water and bring to boil and simmer for 40 minutes.

Crunchy Dessert

1 cup of jumbo oat flakes, ½ cup w.w.flour, ¼ cup almonds, 4 tablespoons corn oil, 2 tablespoons apple juice concentrate, 1 cup raisins.

Combine all ingredients and bake in oven at medium heat for 40 minutes.

Custard

Soya milk, vanilla essence, maple syrup (or corn & barley syrup), kuzu dissolved in cold water.

Mix all and heat.

Cous Cous

1½ cups cous cous   *¾ cup dried fruit*   *3½ cups water*

Cook fruit in water. Dry roast cous cous, add to fruit and set with agar agar powder.

Topping:

cashew nut cream.

Edy	*Aged 12*	*From London*
Florence	*Aged 8*	
Lily	*Aged 5*	
Douglas	*Aged 2*	

Split-Pea Soup (Enough for 4-6 people)

1½ cups green split-peas   *6-7 cups water*

1½" piece of kombu   *1 medium-large onion (diced small)*

½ cup daikon radish or carrot (diced small)
or ½ cup dried daikon (soaked in a little water for 10 minutes and diced)

1 cup celery (diced small)
or Chinese cabbage (diced small)

¼ cup fresh peas (if in season)   *1½ teaspoons light miso*

3 teaspoons ume-su seasoning

1 cup whole-wheat croutons (optional)

½ cup diced smoked tofu (optional)

Watercress or parsley to garnish

Cook split-peas with kombu and water until half cooked (20-30 minutes). In a second pot, layer vegetables (except celery or peas), and put split peas on top. Continue to cook until split- peas are soft (another 20-30 minutes). Add celery and/or peas and simmer for a further 5 minutes. Add seasonings (adding a vinegar helps to balance the "mealy" taste of peas and beans), and allow to be absorbed — 5-10 minutes on a low flame.

This soup is delicious served with croutons made by deep frying or pan frying squares of whole wheat bread, and also by adding smoked tofu. Serve with a garnish such as finely chopped parsley or watercress.

Many children do not like to eat vegetables. A soup is an excellent way to hide vegetables, and thus ensure that children receive the necessary nutrients they contain.

Seed Nut Balls

1 cup lightly roasted sunflower seeds

1 cup lightly roasted pumpkin seeds

½ lightly roasted sesame seeds

1 cup of broken up pieces of rice cake (3 rice cakes) or popcorn

½ cup lightly roaster almonds   *½ cup raisins (optional)*

½ cup barleymalt or corn and barley malt or rice honey.

½ teaspoon natural vanilla essence (optional)

Mix together all the lightly roasted nuts and seeds with the rice cake or popcorn and raisins (if used). In a small pan heat the grain syrup until it bubbles. Add vanilla if used. Pour over the seed mixture and mix thoroughly. Spread on to a baking tray and bake in a pre-heated oven (medium-high) for 5 minutes, until it just starts to go golden on the top. Remove and allow to cool enough to handle. With moist hands form into balls. When these balls cool they become crisp.

Seeds and nuts contain lots of nourishment for children. They are a good source of unsaturated oil, protein and minerals. They are great to use a a snack food.

Tofu Carrot "Sandwitches" (makes about 6)

1 block of organic tofu   *1 medium large carrot*

1" piece of kombu   *½ cup water*   *1 shiitake mushroom*

1-2 teaspoons of shoyu   *1 teaspoon rice wine (optional)*

½ sheet of nori (toasted and cut into strips ¾" wide)

1-2 teaspoons sesame oil

Soak shiitake mushroom (if used) and kombu in the water for 15 minutes. Cut carrot into large slices and simmer in the water with kombu and shitake until tender (but not too soft). Slice the tofu into ¼" slices and pan fry in sesame oil until golden and slightly crispy. Shoyu can be sprinkled on the tofu before the end of frying for a more savoury taste. Blot on paper towels. Taking two pieces of tofu make a sandwich with several pieces of carrot for the filing, and bind round the centre with a strip of nori, dampening the end with water to stick it down.

Children need protein to help them to grow, and the protein from vegetable sources, such as beans, grains, nuts and seeds, is easier to digest than that from animal foods, and contains less saturated fat.

Tofu is a useful food to use sometimes for children as it is rich in protein and calcium, and it is quick and easy to prepare.

ℋazelnut Biscuits

250 grams lightly roasted hazelnuts (save a few whole ones for decorating biscuits)

50 grams brown flour   75 grams whole-wheat pastry flour

1 pinch sea salt

½cup rice honey or other grain sweetener

¾cup apple or pear juice

Grind hazelnuts in a blender into a fine meal. Mix together with flours and salt. Combine rice honey and juice and stir until completely mixed. Pour over the nut/flour mixture and stir gently until the mixture is a smooth batter. Drop spoonfuls onto an oiled baking tray and flatten with a spoon. Decorate each with a whole nut in the centre. Bake in a moderate oven for about 20 minutes, until golden at the edges. Allow to cool on baking rack before serving. This recipe can also be adapted using almond meal instead of hazelnuts.

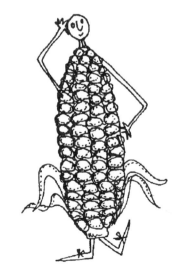

Ellen	*Aged 12*	*From Wirral*
Robert	*Aged 9*	
Gwyneth	*Aged 6*	
John	*Aged 3*	
Nathan	*Aged 7 months*	

Aduki Bean Burgers

½ cup of aduki beans   *6" piece of kombu or wakame*

1 onion — peeled and sliced lengthwise

½lb.carrots or parsnips — scrubbed and sliced

Green vegetables — spring cabbage, kale, watercress.

Small amount of shoyu   *Maize meal or porridge oats*

Wash and soak beans and seaweed. Cook beans, seaweed onion and carrots together until soft and liquid is absorbed. Remove seaweed and chop up small. Return to pan and mash everything together with a potato masher. Lightly steam the green vegetable until bright green. (Watercress only for about ½ minute). Then chop finely and add to the mashed beans and vegetables. Season with shoyu and then add enough maize meal or porridge oats to form a consistency dry enough to form into burgers, but not too dry. (About ¾ - 1cup). Form into burgers (easier with a burger press), and shallow fry in a small amount of oil.

Alternatively instead of adding maize meal or porridge oats put mixture in a casserole (need not be mashed). Then mix together porridge oats, sunflower seeds and sesame oil with a little sea salt to make a crumble topping. Place on top of the aduki bean mixture and bake in oven Mark 4 for about 20 minutes until lightly browned.

Daisy   *Aged 2*   *From Essex*

Savoury Tofu on Rice

Rice — cooked — enough for 4 persons

1 block tofu — marinated in shoyu/ginger — cubed

1 medium onion — sliced

4oz mushrooms — sliced (optional but tasty)

2 large carrots   *2 cups cauliflower florets*

2 cups broccoli pieces   *2 cups water*

2 teaspoons arrowroot/kuzu   *1 sheet nori — toasted*

Shoyu to taste

Prepare all vegetables. Saute onion in a little sesame oil. Steam carrots, broccoli and cauliflower. Add tofu to onions and brown gently. Add mushrooms to onions and tofu. Prepare water and arrowroot/kuzu. Season with a little shoyu. When mushrooms are nearly cooked add arrowroot/kuzu mixture and stir well. Add all other steamed vegetables, and continue to stir until mixture thickens.

Serve on a bed of rice and sprinkle with crumbled nori.

It takes a little practice to time rice, steamed vegetables and saute mix to finish cooking at approximately the same time.

Marloes   *Aged 4*   *From Ipswich*

Oat and Raisin Cookies

1 cup porridge oats   *1 cup 85% flour*

Pinch of salt   *1 teaspoon cinnamon*

1 grated apple   *½cup chopped and roasted hazelnuts*

½ raisins   *4 tablespoons corn oil*

Few drops vanilla   *Apple or pear juice and water*

Mix the first five ingredients together. Add oil and rub in well. Add hazelnuts, raisins and vanilla. Add apple juice with water until you have a firm dough. Spread it on a tray and press firmly. Bake in oven for 30 minutes on mark 5 gas. Cut the biscuits when still hot. Best eaten the same day, which suits most children.

Noodley Miso Soup

2 pints of water	*10cms. wakame*
1 carrot	*½packet tofu*
animal shaped noodles	*Other vegetables like cauliflower etc.*
Cook together for about 10 minutes.	

Add 1-2 tablespoons of white miso.

Henry   *Aged 16*   *From Cambridge*

Oat Porridge and Toasted Nori Seaweed

For two people.

1 mug of oat flakes *— organically grown*	*2.5 mugs of filtered water*
Small pinch of sea salt	*2 sheets of nori seaweed*

Bring the first three items to the boil while stirring, lower the flame and simmer for 5-10 minutes stirring between other breakfast tasks. (If stirring is skimped there are complaints that 'not enough love has been put into the porridge'.)

The sheets of nori are passed back and forth over the gas flame to toast, a few cms. above the flame, and then torn into squares. The dish is then eaten in a way special to adolescents, which is apparently both delicious and idiosyncratic, namely using the lower part of the nori square to scoop up a portion of porridge and folding the top over to form a sandwich which can then deftly be popped into the mouth with fingers.

N.B. This dish may be considered too fattening for teenage girls to eat regularly.

Tina   *Aged 7*   *From Essex*
Michael   *Aged 6*

Chickpeas with Carrots and Cauliflower

½ cup cooked chickpeas — organic   ¼ cauliflower

2 small to medium carrot — organic   3" strip kombu

Miso Sauce:

1 teaspoon miso   1 teaspoon rice vinegar

1 teaspoon kuzu

½ cup of stock from chickpeas, carrots and cauliflower or spring water

Place kombu in saucepan with ½" water. Put in carrots and cauliflower on top of carrots (cauliflower will be out of water). Bring to boil and simmer until done. Dice kombu and return to saucepan together with chickpeas and mix. Dissolve kuzu in a little cold water, add to stock with miso and vinegar, stir over a low flame until thickened and mix with beans and vegetables.

Noodles with Carrots and Sweetcorn

1 cup cooked noodles, wholewheat macaroni

2 carrots cut in half moons or matchsticks

1 corn cob, or tin of natural unadulterated sweetcorn kernels

Cook the cob for 15 minutes and remove kernels. Carrots can be used raw or sauteed until just tender but still crisp.

Mix noodles, carrots and sweetcorn together and add dressing:-

1 umeboshi plum finely chopped   ½ diced onion

Mix together in suribachi, and add 1 tablespoon tahini. Add water a little at a time until it reaches the consistency of mayonnaise.

Quick Cous Cous Cake

½ cup spring water   ½ cup organic apple juice

Handful of raisins   21 Hunza apricots

1 cup cous cous

Soak apricots for a few hours or over night. Throw away soaking water and add fresh to cover, simmer until cooked. Strain off juice and put in saucepan together with spring water and apple juice. Wash raisins and add to pan. Bring to boil and simmer for a few minutes. Meanwhile put apricots through a sieve using a rice paddle. Save stones. Add one cup of cous cous to pan and stir until thickened. Remove to flan dish and when cool top with pureed apricots. The kernels from the apricots can be used to decorate the cake, or saved for mum.

Lentil Picnic Bake

½ cup lentils   1 large or 2 small carrots diced or sliced

3" strip kombu   1 bay leaf

¼teaspoon sweet basil   1 medium onion diced or sliced

½ cup cooked quinnoa   1 teaspoon miso

1 heaped tablespoon of chopped parsley

Put first six ingredients in pan and add spring water. Bring to boil and simmer until cooked. Remove from heat, mix in miso and parsley, then add cooked quinnoa and mix thoroughly. Add a little water if too dry. Put in baking dish at mark 4 for 30 minutes. Sprinkle with roasted sesame seeds.

Tikam Berry   *Aged 6*   *From America*

Lemon Pie

1½ cups apple juice   *3 teaspoons agar agar*

pinch salt   *½ cup cold apple juice*

2 teaspoons kuzu   *Juice and rinds of 1½-2 lemons (to taste)*

Rice syrup to taste   *Vanilla*

Pre-baked (15-20 mins.) pie shell

Simmer 1½ cups apple juice and agar agar until melted. Add pinch of salt. Mix kuzu with ½ cup cold apple juice, bring to the boil, stir until thick. Add to apple/agar.
Add lemon, and rice syrup. Take off heat and add vanilla. Pour into pie shell. Oven gas mark 6 for 30 minutes.

Alternatives to Lemon:

Blueberries, strawberries, blackberries or raspberries.
Filling can be put in pudding dishes and set in refrigerator without baking.

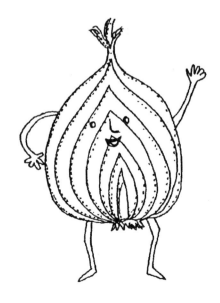

Shanti	*Aged 15*	*From Devon*
Rowan	*Aged 12*	
Ewan	*Aged 8*	
Morwenna	*Aged 6*	
Meryl	*Aged 5*	

Red Sauce (For 4-6 people)

(40 minutes preparation and cooking time)

8oz. red lentils — rinsed and soaked for 2-4 hours

1lb. pumpkin (Hokkaido/butternut) cut into small cubes ½" approx.

1lb. carrots cut same as for pumpkin

Few pieces of dulse 1/8 cup approx. Cleaned, soaked and cut into small pieces

1-2 tablespoons shoyu (depending on the age of the children) Can add 1 spoon — cook — remove childrens helpings and then add the other spoonful.

½ bunch parsley (optional)

Juice of 1 lemon

2 cups water — possibly 3 will be needed

Add the following to a heavy bottomed pan — dulse with soaking water, lentils minus soaking water, pumpkin and carrots and water. Bring to boil over moderate high flame. Reduce flame so that it simmers to gentle boil. Cook for 20 minutes. Lentils should have passed the light fluffy stage and be thickening up. Add shoyu and cook another 10 minutes on as low a flame as possible.
Add lemon juice and parsley and stir in well.
If you have very young children I find they prefer this blended. Any leftovers turn into a soup with a cup or two of water added.

Ginger Pear Kuzu (4-6 people)

(25-30 mins. preparation and cooking time)

8oz. pear juice concentrate / 1 litre pear juice

2lbs. pears — cut into 4

2" piece of ginger — grated — the juice of to be used, maybe less for little ones

2-3 teaspoons kuzu/arrowroot — diluted in cold water

1 teaspoon sea salt — less for little ones

Water — 1 cup if not using concentrate /1 litre if using concentrate

¼ jar sesame spread/roasted tahini diluted and pureed in 1 cup of water

Put pear juice, water, ginger juice and salt in a pan and bring to the boil over medium high flame. Add quartered pears. Cook until tender over medium flame — approx. 5-15 minutes. Add diluted kuzu/arrowroot and sesame spread. Stir very gently and constantly until thick and consistently so. Remove from pan and place in serving dish. Depending on family's likes you may want to make the sauce thicker or thinner, more or less ginger.

Fish Spread (4-6 people)

(10 mins. preparation)

2 medium size tins sardines/tuna/salmon — I include the oil — up to you

Juice of ½ -1 lemon

½ jar/4oz. approx. sunflower mayonnaise

Small amount of finely chopped parsley (optional)

Puree in large suribachi fish, lemon juice and mayonnaise. (Add half lemon juice, put some aside for the children, then add the remainder). Mix well. Add parsley if using.

We eat this spread with pitta bread and various salads and some raw vegetable sticks.

This is a convenience dish in our family that we have approximately once a month — more in winter. All my children love this. While they won't eat any fish purees made with fresh fish, they love tinned fish.

Humous (4-6 people)

(3-4 hours prep. and cooking time)

8oz. chickpeas — soaked over night or all day

4oz. sesame spread/roasted tahini or tahini pureed with 1 cup of cooking water

Juice of 2 lemons

4" piece of kombu — thoroughly rinsed

2 tablespoons vegetable oil — sunflower, corn or olive

2 cloves of garlic —finely crushed

Water — approx. 4 cups, maybe more

2 tablespoons shoyu

½bunch parsley for garnish

Strain off soaking water. Add kombu to the bottom of pressure cooker, chickpeas and water. Pressure cook for 2-3 hours. Check hourly to see how much water there is. There should always be enough to cover. Cook the chickpeas until they have split open. This makes for a much more tender,

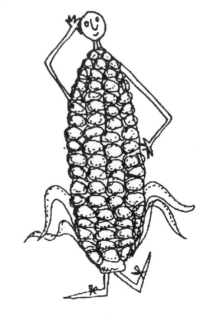

delicious, easy to digest humous. When they are that tender add the shoyu and cook for another 20 minutes. Save some chickpeas that are cooked for decoration — make star shape. The mixture can be pureed in either a suribachi or blender, with the garlic and lemon juice.

We eat humous hot or cold with vegetable cous cous and a green salad. We have it cold with pitta bread or chappattis and various salads and raw vegetable sticks.

All my children love this, especially my most fussy child, because it is rich and satisfying.

Emma   Aged 7½   *From Somerset*

Sarah   Aged 4

Emma and Sarah enjoy whole grain as the centre of their meal. The following dishes are some of the foods they like to eat with the grain.

Tofu with Onions and Corn

½ block fresh tofu, cut in small cubes

½ block smoked tofu, cut in small cubes

2 onions diced   *1 cup cooked corn*

Few drops shoyu — few drops sesame oil

Heat pan, add a few drops of sesame oil, add onions.
Saute uncovered for 3 minutes. Add a few drops of shoyu. Add both kinds of tofu, cover, cook gently for 5-7 minutes. (If sticks add small amount of water.) Add cooked corn, mix well and serve.

Dulse Salad

1 cup dulse, washed, soaked for 4-5 minutes cut into small pieces

2 tangerines, cut small pieces   *½ cup cucumber, diced*

1 tablespoon roasted seeds   *1 tablespoon apple juice concentrate*

Few drops shoyu

Place dulse in a serving bowl. Add rest of the ingredients, mix well. Serve.

Green Rolls

Steamed or boiled greens (kale, spring greens, watercress or brussel sprout tops)

2 sheets toasted nori

½ cup sauerkraut (squeeze excess juice before using)

Gently squeeze cooked greens before using. Cut the stems and keep separately. Place one sheet of toasted nori on top of a sushi mat. (Shiny part on the outside). Cover with 2-3 layers of the cooked greens. Lay the separated stems in the centre, together with some sauerkraut.

From the bottom (near you), start rolling up the nori around the ingredients, pressing it firmly. When completed, seal the nori with a few drops of water. Cut with a sharp knife into at least 6 pieces each roll.

Instead of sauerkraut, you can use a variety of ingredients, like cooked tofu or tempeh, hiziki or arame, or some softly cooked vegetables.

Tempeh "fingers"

1 block tempeh — defrosted

Mugi miso or white miso (for lighter sweeter taste)

Slice the block of tempeh in half. Place one half on plate.

Cover the piece with a thin layer of miso, all it's sides, top and bottom. Add the next piece on top and proceed as previously.

Leave in the fridge for around 20-24 hours.

Remove all the miso and keep for making dressing,sauces etc.

Rinse each piece of tempeh under cold water, to clean off any remaining miso. Leave to drain. Slice each piece of tempeh, in a desired shape. Heat frying pan, add some sesame oil, and pan fry each piece both sides. (No need to add any extra seasoning).

Serve for older children, with diluted natural mustard and water.

If children are very small, use white miso instead of mugi miso.

Cauliflower Soup

½ small cauliflower	*1 strip kombu*
1 onion, diced	*1 bayleaf*
Wholewheat pasta shapes	*2 drops toasted sesame oil*
White miso to taste	

Bring water to boil, add diced onions.

Add strip of kombu, bayleaf,pasta, cauliflower (cut in small florets). Cover and cook for 10-15 minutes. Add two drops of toasted sesame oil (for richer taste), and season to taste with white miso. Reduce flame, simmer gently for two minutes.

Remove strip of kombu for further use (cook beans) before serving.

Nori Tempura

2 sheets nori, cut into rectangles (1"x 3")approx.

Sesame oil for deep frying

Batter:

4 tablespoon wholewheat flour   *Pinch sea salt*

1 tablespoon arrowroot   *Sparkling water*

Combine all the dry ingredients for the batter, then add enough sparkling water to give a thick consistency. Leave to stand for ½ hour, ideally in a refrigerator. Heat 2-3 inches of oil in a pan (do not smoke it). Drop a small piece of batter into the oil, if it sinks and rises up on the surface it means the oil is ready to use.

Take one strip of nori at a time, and dip it into the batter. Drop it into the oil turning it and cook for 1-2 minutes until it turns golden brown.

Drain on a paper towel. Serve hot.

In order to help to digest oil, serve with some slices of lemon, or mustard diluted with water and a few drops of shoyu. Children don't always like to use grated daikon with shoyu or ginger.

Light Daikon/Carrot Pickles

1 cup daikon, cut in thin pieces   *1 cup carrots, cut in thin pieces*

Sea salt   *Filtered water*

Place vegetables in a glass jar. Mix filter water (cold) with sea salt, to have a similar taste to sea water.

Pour the liquid into the jar with the vegetables. The liquid should completely cover the vegetables. Cover with a cheese cloth and keep it in a cool dark place for 5 days (avoid using the fridge). After the fifth day the pickles can be eaten. Close the jar with a proper lid and store it in the fridge or cool place.

This is the most simple way to make pickles. Enjoy changing to different vegetables. It is a very good way for children to eat daikon.

Baked Beans

Haricot beans (soaked overnight)   1 strip kombu

1 cup red cabbage or beetroot, cut in small pieces

Seasonings:

mugi miso   *Freshly squeezed ginger juice*

Umeboshi plum or vinegar

Apple juice concentrate or corn & barley syrup.
Discard soaking water. Place beans in a pressure cooker with a strip of kombu,
red cabbage or beetroot and water, (1½ water/1 beans).
Bring to pressure, cook till soft (approx. 45 mins.) Add seasonings to taste, in
small amounts to find the right taste.

Quick Water Saute Greens

Any kind of strong green (kale, spring green) finely cut

½ cup mung bean sprouts

Few drops shoyu, and a few drops rice vinegar (to taste)

Heat a light stainless steel pan, add 2-3 tablespoons of water.
Add the greens, and a few drops of shoyu, stir constantly for 3-4 minutes
(depending on the kind of greens, some will take a few minutes longer). Switch
off, add sprouts and a few drops of rice vinegar. (Optional). Serve.

Lemon Jelly

2 cups water

Pinch sea salt

3-4 tablespoons agar agar flakes

1 tablespoon lemon rind

½ tablespoon sesame butter or tahini

Corn/barley malt or regular barley malt

⅓ cup apple juice concentrate

Some good quality biscuits

Place biscuits on the bottom of a mould. Bring the water to the boil, and add
the rest of the ingredients, except the tahini. Simmer for 5-7 minutes. Add the
tahini (diluted first with a small amount of the cooking liquid).
After cooking pour the liquid into the mould. Leave it to set for 2-3 hours.

Snacky Mix

½ cup roasted pumpkin seeds	*½ cup roasted sunflower seeds*
½ cup sultanas	*1 toasted nori sheet*

Mix nuts and sultanas in a bowl.

Cut toasted nori into small pieces. Mix with the rest of ingredients.

Aoife	*Aged 10*	*From Ireland*
Ckodhna	*Aged 5*	

Minestrone

6oz. haricot beans, soaked overnight	*1 onion chopped*
2 cloves garlic, finely chopped or crushed	*2 carrots, diced*
1 leek, sliced	*1 courgette, diced (optional)*
1 small head white cabbage, shredded or chopped finely	*2 stalks celery, chopped*
1 tin chopped tomatoes or tomato puree	*8oz. short pasta (e.g. macaroni)*
Short strip kombu	*Handful dulse, washed*
1 tablespoon mugi miso	*Parsley, chopped finely*
Grated Parmesan cheese (optional)	

Strain beans and place in pot with strip of kombu, from which the salt has been wiped. Cover with double quantity of cold water and bring to the boil. Boil for 10 minutes with lid off. Cover and simmer for 40-50 minutes. (With pressure cooking they tend to go to pieces). They should be tinged with pink when cooked. Gently saute onion and garlic in a little oil. (Cold-pressed olive oil for authenticity). Add carrots, courgette and leek. Cook for 5 minutes more. Cover with water or vegetable stock and add tomatoes with juice. Add dulse. Bring to boil and simmer until carrots are barely cooked. Add cabbage and celery. Bring back to boil. Add pasta, or cook separately and add. (The secret of adding in pasta to cook in the minestrone, is to have a very large pot and a kettle of hot water ready to top up and cover everything at each successive stage). After 10 minutes check that pasta is cooked and switch off heat. Add cooked beans and miso — diluted in some of the soup, and leave to sit for a further 5 minutes or so, covered to retain heat. Chop parsley and add or serve separately to sprinkle on top. For authenticity also supply a small bowl of grated Parmesan cheese. Sometimes we have wholemeal garlic bread with it as a treat.

Golden Millet Croquettes

Cooked millet, whether on its own or with onions and/or other vegetables — it can be a way to sneak in a few vegetables unnoticed.

| Carrots, grated | Tahini | Shoyu or salt |
| Fine oatmeal — optional | Water | Parsley — optional |

Pre-heat oven to Gas 5, 375F, 190C.
In a bowl, mix cooked millet, tahini, salt/shoyu, grated carrots and a little water until the mixture holds together. (I often find a little oatmeal helps to bind it, along with the tahini and water).
Form into little balls and place on an oiled baking tray. I find my kids like to oil the baking tray using a pastry brush (or they could use clean fingers!) and also making the balls using an icecream scoop. Bake in oven until golden — 20 minutes. The carrots give them a lovely golden colour. Serve with a bean dish of your choice.

Deep-Fried Carrot Tops

I am always trying to find ways to get my children to eat greens and this is one they love. So we have them quite often for the short time the tops of organically grown carrots are available.

Make a batter with wholemeal flour, water and a pinch of salt. Dip in carrot tops and drop — carefully — into hot oil one or two at a time, depending on size. When crisp, drain on kitchen paper, then serve immediately. I like a drop of tamari on mine, but the children eat them straight.

Sauteed Mushrooms

We like mushrooms that have opened, rather than button mushrooms, as they have more flavour. Sautee in cold-pressed corn oil and when just cooked add a dash of tamari.

Tahini on Toast

For people who eat sourdough bread and like tahini, this might prove a handy snack. Toast slice of sourdough bread on one side. Turn over and spread with tahini on other side. Toast again until bubbling and browned.

Rhubarb Crumble

I usually use Hunza apricots as a sweetener to cook in with rhubarb. But if you still find rhubarb too acid, you can make "mock rhubarb" imitative in flavour and colour, by cooking hunza apricots with a few umeboshi plums. Expensive, but good in terms of flavour and nourishment.

We love rhubarb crumble. Crumble made with fine oatmeal, sometimes mixed with wholemeal flour, water, corn oil or sunflower margarine and date syrup or barley malt. Serve it with Provamel Vanilla Soya Dessert, which does contain sugar I'm afraid, in lieu of custard.

Part II
Weaning Advice

The following guidelines are based on my own, and other mother's experience. There are no hard and fast rules. Each mother usually knows her own child best, and weaning becomes a dance between mother and child with no fixed steps.

It is usual to start supplementing breast-milk around six months. Obviously the appearance of teeth can be an indicator. By around one year a full range of foods should be included in the baby's diet, and the weaning process is best completed by eighteen months. If you leave complete weaning until after eighteen months, you will find the child's own will-power has come into play and so the process becomes more difficult. Cold sage tea will help dry up milk. It is advisable to gradually reduce feeds with a reduction of liquid intake by the mother.

Before the weaning stage a mother may find she has no milk, or due to unforeseen circumstances she has to stop breast feeding. Don't feel guilty. There are plenty of other ways to express your love. With experienced advice and knowledge you may be able to use grain milk with beans; or corn milk. There is no need to reach the stage of despair because there are perfectly suitable soyamilk based formulas available from the chemist. Goats milk is closer to human milk, but can make children stubborn and irritable.

It is said that children who reject milk at an early age are often more intellectually inclined. By the age of two years children's stomach enzymes change, adjusting to suit the digestion of solids. They can no longer digest milk satisfactorily.

The general outline to introducing foods is as follows:-

4-6 months	cereal	no salt, use grain sweeteners
5-7 months	vegetables	no salt, use grain sweeteners
8 months	beans	no salt, use grain sweeteners
8-12 months	fish	
12 months +	fruit	(summertime)

Two important points to keep in mind when weaning:-

1. Breast milk is naturally sweet, so do use high quality grain- based sweeteners and naturally sweet vegetables. When appropriate, use some cooked fruit.

2. As soon as you decrease the amount of milk it is important to give the baby adequate amounts of oil to help maintain body weight. Ground roasted seeds (pumpkin, sunflower, sesame) are the best source of oil in the early days.

The combination of oil and sweetness prevents cravings that could otherwise lead to an insatiable appetite for rice and other grains which can in turn contribute to bloating and overloading of the digestive system.

Here are the basic weaning recipes:-

Grain Milk and Baby Rice

⅓ cup brown rice

⅓ cup sweet rice

⅓ cup barley or oats

1" kombu (sea vegetable)

10 cups water

1 tablespoon roasted sesame seeds — very finely ground

Grain sweetener — rice syrup, corn & barley, barley& malt

Stage I   Age 4-6 months

Wash grains, bring first five ingredients slowly to the boil, then simmer for 1½-2 hours until the liquid is creamy. Strain liquid through muslin or a sieve. Add ground sesame to the strained liquid. Add grain sweetener to flavour. Feed on a spoon — preferably wooden.

Stage II   Age 6-7 months

As above with only 7 cups of water. When cooked put through a hand blender/Mouli. This makes a puree and the blender retains the grain husks, (Mothercare sell this type of blender for babies). At this stage you can add 8-10 pre-soaked aduki or soya beans to cook with the grain.

Stage III Age 8-10 months

As above but reducing the water to 5 cups. When cooked use a baby mill. This will grind up the whole grain into a puree for the baby. Cannon make these baby mills. (Available from Clearspring — address at back of book). They are an invaluable piece of baby equipment.

Stage IV Age one year

As above — reducing water to 4 cups. Grind in a suribachi.

Stage V Age 18 months

As above — reducing to 3 cups of water. Serve as a whole grain.

The above stages are a rough guideline. Please use your own initiative, and let your baby guide you as to when to move on to each stage. Some mothers prefer to continue grinding food until the baby has got it's own back teeth for grinding it's grain. Also in some traditions the mother chews the grain to give the baby. But a mother's saliva, although able to help digestion, may be too salty. It may be appropriate for one mouthful per meal (like adults eating a little pickle), but not for all the baby's food.

Vegetables

Soft cooked and pureed. Introduce one vegetable at a time. You can add ground roasted seeds or occasionally vegetables sauteed in sunflower oil before pureeing. This adds that important oil. Start with soft unpureed pieces at about 9-10 months.

Sea Vegetables

Kombu is used from the beginning to cook with the grain, and then in cooking beans. 9-10 months add nori flakes to the diet. 10-11 months dulse and arame can be added, usually cooked with vegetables.
At 1 year use all types of sea vegetables.

Beans

Tofu, green split peas, tempeh, red lentils are all suitable choices to start with. By 9-10 months also chick peas. Cook with a little kombu until soft then puree. The kombu adds important minerals to the diet, which contributes to healthy bone formation, and other vital processes.
(My children did not enjoy beans until I added some miso or shoyu for flavour. Add this at the last ten minutes of the cooking time).

Fish

Can be added into a soup, or steamed and mashed with soft rice. If you introduce fish during the summer, then start also with some cooked fruit to balance the fish.

Fruit

Simmer fresh fruit (i.e. apples, pears) until soft, then puree. Half a pinch of salt will help balance the acidity of the fruit.
Beans and fruit do not digest well together, so in the beginning give them on separate days.

Drinks

Water.
Bancha tea and barley malt.
Vegetable liquid

Teething Biscuits

These should be more chewable than breakable. Mix wholewheat flour with barley malt and water to make a dough. (Use freshly ground flour when possible). Bake slowly in the oven.

Baby food should be cooked on a medium or low flame.

Enjoy the weaning dance!

Part III
Balanced Meals for Children

First the dance and now the balancing act!

Exactly what is a balanced diet for children?

Not an easy question to answer. I took the standard Macrobiotic Diet, and altered the ratios a bit, because children's needs are different from adults.

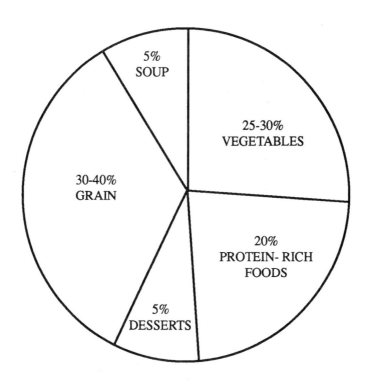

Let us take each portion of this pie and find out what is in it.

30%-40% Grain

There are over twenty three different grains or grain based products available to use. (Basic cooking times are in the appendix). Whole grains are an essential part of the diet, and together with beans, seeds or nuts contain all the amino acids to make a complete protein for those not wanting to use animal foods.

The beauty of whole grains is that they are a live food, a seed which can grow into an abundant plant, even after being stored for years. The grinding and refining of grains take away not only essential vitamins and minerals but also that special life energy children need to help them grow.

Most, but not all, children enjoy soft cooked rice, normally plain, but some love to have something special on top, like sauteed breadcrumbs, roasted seeds, or condiments made from baked and ground sea vegetables. Barley is a grain which suits the energy of children: it is nice cooked in winter stews. Sweetcorn is a summertime grain, whereas noodles or pasta seem to be the number one favourite of all children, and can be served in many different ways. Try a sauce of pureed root vegetables with tofu cheese grated on top as a quick and easy lunch. In the summer use as a salad dish: mix pasta shapes with boiled vegetables, deep fried tofu and roasted seeds with a rice vinegar dressing. Added to soups is another favourite. Remember though that pasta alone will not meet all the requirements that whole grain can give children. Bread is best used only occasionally, as it tends to block and congest, and is not easy to digest. To help overcome this you can try steaming it.

5% Soup

Sixty five percent of our body is water, so soups provide an excellent way to take liquid. Thick soups in winter, and clear broths in summer.

Soups are normally seasoned with sea salt or salty fermented products such as miso or shoyu, since good quality sea salt has a mineral profile similar to that of human blood. Of course young children need less salt than adults, and babies none. So remove their soup from the pot before you season.

Children often prefer the lighter taste of sweet white miso instead of strong dark miso. Miso is an excellent fermented product that aids in the digestion and assimilation of foods. Along with miso or shoyu for seasoning sea vegetables make good soup stocks. Kombu in particular. Other sea vegetables, along with the whole range of vegetables, make delicious soups. Grain and bean soups are good in winter, or as a meal in themselves. Always save vegetable cooking water to use in soup making.

25% — 30% Vegetables

Children definitely have a love/hate relationship with some or occasionally all vegetables.

Vegetables tend to fall into three main categories. Root vegetables that grow downwards, rounded vegetables, and upward growing leafy vegetables. It is good to include something from each category. You may have to use all your imagination and ingenuity to include them on a regular basis. Try different cooking styles — boiling, steaming, baking (not for babies or very young), sauteeing, frying (very popular — especially dipped in a batter first), pickled, pureed in soups, raw, large pieces, small pieces, flower shapes, animal shapes, put in pies or cakes (carrot is the most popular, or try parsnips), sweetened with barley malt.

Vegetables contain a large number of vitamins and minerals needed for children's growth. The best you can buy are organic or those grown by biodinamic or permaculture methods. You may even consider growing some vegetables yourself. Young children enjoy growing their own food. Radishes are excellent as they grow quickly, need little space, and can be eaten raw or best blanched for two minutes. Cook them whole — leaves as well — season with salt in the cooking or sprinkle on umeboshi vinegar after cooking.

The following are some of the vegetables mainly native to this country, and most regularly used:

ROOT	ROUND	LEAFY
Downward energy		*Upward energy*
Parsnip	Cauliflower	Broccoli
Carrot	Leek	Brussels Sprout
Daikon (Mouli)	Spring Onion	and Tops
Burdock	Onion	Bok Choy
Dandelion Root	Pumpkin & Squash	Cabbage
Salsify	Radish	Chinese Cabbage
	Swede	Daikon Greens
	Turnip	Dandelion Greens
	Cucumber	Kale
	Marrow	Nettle Tops
		Watercress
		Pea
		Mustard Greens
		Parsley
		Turnip Greens
		Mushroom
		Runner Bean

Sea Vegetables

They can be cooked as a dish in their own right, or included in soups, or used in preparing grain and bean dishes. They are very high in vitamins, minerals, and trace elements. In fact half a sheet of toasted nori a day would be more beneficial than any vitamin or mineral pills or supplements you may be persuaded by popular media to give your children. Oil used in the cooking of sea vegetables will add richness and smoothly facilitate the absorption of minerals by children.

Varieties include:

Arame	Hijiki	Kombu (Kelp)
Wakame	Dulse	Nori prepared sheets
Purple Nori	Grockle	

20% Protein Rich Foods

Children need far more protein rich foods than adults, as they are still growing. As already mentioned, beans served along with grains will provide all the amino acids to make a complete protein. It is recommended to cook beans with sea vegetables, as they add minerals to the beans. Normally used is a strip (6") of kombu or wakame. Salt is not added to beans until the last 10-15 minutes of cooking time. This also aids in their digestibility. A wide variety of beans can be used for children, and their cooking times are in the appendix. Children love tofu and tempeh — soya bean products — which are convenient for cooking in a variety of ways.

Normally in a Macrobiotic diet we do include fish. For children growing in our damp grey climate in Britain, fish (especially oily fish) is important, not only for protein, but also vitamin B_{12}. The lack of this vitamin, which is needed only in very small amounts, is very harmful to children's growth. (Adults can store it for up to five years). So if you follow a Vegan diet you may need to give supplements. Four day old sprouted beans and grain should contain some B_{12}. Generally though children enjoy fish, and it is a very beneficial food for them. It also provides vitamin D during the winter months for children.

FISH TYPES INCLUDE:

Herring	Cod	Mackerel
Bass	Sardine	Plaice
Tuna	Sprat	Halibut
Salmon	Turbot	Sole

Animal meats are not necessary for children's healthy growth, but we do not need to exclude them entirely. Organically fed and naturally reared chicken would be more suitable than wild game such as pheasant, rabbit etc. Quality is very important. Let the child's own judgment determine if they want to eat some meat or not. Do not force it on them.

If your child refuses to eat fish or meat, and you are concerned about their getting enough B_{12}, then try some live yoghurt. One tablespoon a day should provide all they need.

Seeds and Nuts

These not only provide protein in the diet, they also are an important source of fat and oil for children, and should be used daily.

Seeds should be lightly toasted and ground, as young children cannot chew them sufficiently.

Nuts also need roasting and chopping or grinding if they cannot be chewed. Children like nuts and seeds as a snack between meals, or as a sprinkle on their grain.

Pumpkin seed	Chestnuts	Sunflower seed
Walnuts	Sesame seed	Almonds
Hazelnuts		

5% Desserts

Well this must be the most popular part of the menu for most children. There is a wide range of foods that can be included in making desserts — grains and grain sweeteners, nuts, seeds,and vegetables along with a wide variety of fruits. Fresh fruits are best locally grown, or from cooler climates like our own, rather than tropical varieties. Dried fruits are also important to include. All fruits are best cooked, and a pinch of salt will help counteract their acidity.

Apples	Melon	Pears
Grapes	Raspberry	Watermelon
Cherry	Apricot	Strawberry
Peach	Raisin	Black/Red/White Currants
Plum	Date	Damson
Sultanas	Gooseberry	

Cakes and biscuits can be sweetened with grain derived sweeteners:
Barley Malt   Rice Syrup   Corn Syrup
Amasake (naturally sweet fermented rice puree)

There are a wide number of fruit juices, spreads, and concentrates now available — many organic — that can be used in sweetening. Also available now, though quite expensive, are a variety of sugar free sweets. These are useful at Christmas, Birthdays, holidays and other special occasions.

Drinks

Children need to drink when they are thirsty, and generally need more liquid than adults, especially when the weather is hot. Water is a good standby at all times. Children's drinks are often sweetened. Ice cold drinks or strong roasted flavoured drinks are best avoided.

Amasake — warmed and diluted   Whole grain milks
                                       — sweetened

Diluted fruit juices   Spring or well water
Non-stimulating herbal teas such as nettle, comfrey, rosehip, camomile, etc. — sweetened.

The above guidelines can act as a framework to work with, but not to get neurotic over! Guide lines based on intellect do not always fit into a child's intuitively felt needs. Their rejection of certain foods, and over indulgence in others, usually reflect instinctive inner needs, which we need to recognise and respect. Children are wonderful — they will only eat what they need, and leave what they do not need. Listen to their cravings, and look for the cause i.e. sweet cravings maybe caused by too much salty cooking. Never force a particular food, for there is always a reason why it is refused.

In encouraging our children to eat a balanced diet, the most influential thing we adults can do is to eat and enjoy a balanced diet ourselves. It is important to try and cook one main meal a day based on the above guidelines, and then sit and eat together as a family. Each individual child and adult can then take more or less of each dish according to their needs.

There are certainly going to be times when your child will not eat a balanced meal, and then you can consider balancing out their food over a day, a week, or even a month or longer.

Also we have to remember that children are basically healthy, and they can eat far more variety, and include foods which we as adults may choose to avoid because of our overindulgence in the past.

A meal does not become non-macrobiotic because we use a little tomato, a few herbs or a sprinkle of cheese. If that is the way your child enjoys eating their grain and vegetable dishes, it is not a major problem. It is more important to have variety and remain flexible.

The most important ingredient we can put in the food is our LOVE. We must also remember that happy healthy children grow because of all aspects of their environment, and not simply the physical food we cook them.

Children thrive in the company of other children, and such contact should be actively promoted. They need regular exercise in the open air and sunlight. They respond to personal attention and play, so do free yourself from the kitchen and play with them. That really is the point of life.

We can only do our best for our children. Sharing with them a way of life which we can only hope they will continue to follow. We cannot create perfect children — they already are.

I hope the information in this section has not overwhelmed you. It is helpful to attend cooking classes, and to talk to other mothers following macrobiotic guidelines in their diet. I have given a few contact addresses at the end of the book.

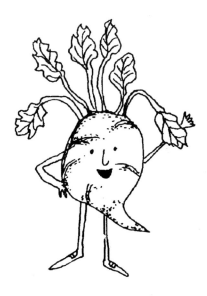

Amazing Grains!

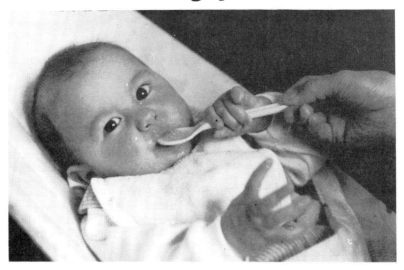

Baby-rice being enjoyed *(recipe page 50)*

Jonathan's birthday cous-cous cake *(recipe page 37)*

Part IV
Kitchen Remedies for
Minor Ailments

Bed Wetting

Make mochi sweet rice — pounded, and then cover balls of pounded mochi in roasted black sesame seeds. Have them at evening meal. Also stop all liquids two hours before bedtime.

Bleeding

If bleeding from a cut is profuse then miso will definitely stop the bleeding, but it will also sting.

Bumps and Bruises

They can be helped by placing tofu or cabbage leaf on, or if you are away from home, a tube of "Bach Flower Rescue Remedy Cream" works wonders. (Keep it at all times in your handbag.)

Burns (Minor)

Cover burn area with cold salty water, or a piece of tofu, until pain goes. Then seal burn with a vegetable oil. A drop of essential oil of lavender in the vegetable oil will aid healing.

Colds

These are actual nature's natural remedy to clear out excesses in the body. To aid the natural process a kuzu drink will help.

4 teaspoons kuzu	*1 pint water*
1 umeboshi plum	

Mix together cold. Then simmer for 20 minutes. Add a drop of shoyu to each ½ cup of liquid.

Cough — Dry

Make a sweet drink with:-

Hot water	*Ginger*
Tangerine skin	*1-2 grains pepper*

Cough — Wet

Make a sweet drink with :-

Hot water	*Barley malt*
Lemon juice	

For both types of cough avoid baked flour and dairy produce.

Cuts and Grazes

Cover with a sheet of Nori. It will stop bleeding and help replace mineral loss.

Insect Bites and Stings

Grate daikon or turnip and squeeze out the juice and apply to the bite. Or rub with a slice of onion.

Nappy Rash

Wash area with warm water, dry, then dust with cornflower and rub on sesame oil.

Cut out fruit from mother's diet if breast feeding or from child's diet.

Stomach Upset

Give only a simple meal of soft rice or rice cream (pureed rice). Umeboshi plums are very good at restoring the acid/alkaline balance in the stomach. I am always amazed at how quickly children can get over stomach ache, especially if their interest is drawn to something they like. If it does persist get a doctor's diagnosis.

Teething

Try rice syrup tea, or shiitake mushroom tea, or a combination.

1 shiitake mushroom   *½ pint water*

Simmer 10-15 minutes. Add rice syrup if required and give on a teaspoon at a warm temperature.
"Weleda" homeopathic teething granules may also help. Rubbing the gums with alcohol is an old remedy (sake or whisky), but you may not want to try this one.

Travel Sickness

Eat some umeboshi plum, or for sea sickness stick a whole plum on the navel. It really does work!

If you tend to worry about your child's growth and health, then try this little health test:-

Is the child growing well?

Does it manage to keep it's feet and hands warm?

Does it have a good appetite?

Is it active?

Is it happy and dynamic?

Does it have good bowel movements with no undigested food?

Does your child sleep well?

If you can answer "yes" to the above — ***stop worrying.***

When children are ill it is important to get a doctor's diagnosis. When you have that diagnosis you can try some of the home remedies described in the book "Macrobiotic Home Remedies" by Mishio Kushi and Mark Van Cauwenbeghe, M.D. A macrobiotic counsellor will also be able to advise you, as should an experienced mother. Remember some childhood illnesses are part of the natural process of growing up.

It is good to know that drugs and medicines do have alternatives, but that does not mean totally excluding western medicine.

Trust your instincts to tell you when to use which option.

Appendix I

Grain Cooking Times

1 cup dry grain	Cups of water	Cooking time in minutes
Pot barley	2½-3	40-60
Whole oats	2½-3	40-60
Brown rice, short grain	1½-2	45-60
Brown rice, long grain	1½-2	45-60
Millet	3-4	35
Buckwheat	3	25
Whole rye grains	3	120
Corn or maize meal (polenta)	4	25-30
Oat, barley & rye flakes	3-4	10-20
Basmati rice	2	10-15
Sweetcorn	to cover	10
Bulgar (use boiling water)	2	15
Cous cous (use boiling water)	1½	4-5
Quinoa	2¼	15
Udon (250gm)	Plenty of boiling water shock with cold water	15

Basic Recipe for Grains

Put the measured dry grain into a cooking pot, fill with cold water, swirl to separate the husks, dust, etc. from the grain, and pour off the water.

Repeat twice. Add the measured quantity of water and sea salt (1pinch to 1 cup of dry grain). Cover, bring to the boil and simmer till all the water is absorbed. Do not stir during cooking.

Rice tastes nicer the larger quantity you cook.

Three cups is a good quantity, and when cooked will keep 4-6 days. Re-use by steaming, frying, in burgers, rice porridge, rice salads etc.

Amazake

Amazake is a natural sweetener made from fermented sweet rice. It can be used as a sweetener for cookies and cakes, pancakes and doughnuts, and in making bread. Amasake can also be blended in a food mill, placed in a saucepan with a pinch of sea salt and a little boiling water, brought to the boil and then served hot or cool as a drink. Especially enjoyed by younger children.

4 cups sweet brown rice   8 cups water

½ cup koji (special bacteria needed to begin fermentation)

Wash rice, drain and soak overnight in 8 cups of water. Place rice in a pressure cooker. Bring to pressure. Reduce flame and cook for 20 minutes. Turn off flame and let the rice sit in pressure cooker for 45 minutes. When the rice is cool enough to handle with your hands, mix in the koji and allow the mixture to ferment at least 4 hours but no longer than 8 hours. Do this by placing the rice and koji in a glass bowl. (Do not use a metal mixing bowl). Cover the bowl with a towel and keep the rice warm during the process of fermentation. This can be done by placing the bowl in an oven with just the pilot light on or keeping it near a radiator. Several times during the period of fermentation mix the ingredients so that the koji will melt. Place rice in a pot, bring to the boil. As soon as it starts to bubble, turn the flame off. Allow to cool. Place rice in a glass bowl or jar and refrigerate.

To keep for a long time, amasake should be cooked over a low flame until it becomes a brown colour.

When using as a sweetener, you may either add as it is to pastries or blend first to make it smooth.

Bean Cooking Times

1 cup dry beans/pulses	Cups of water	Simmering time
Aduki beans	3-4	1½-2 hours
Chick peas (garbanzos)	3-4	3 hours
Brown/green lentils	3-4	1 hour
Black/red kidney beans	4	1½-2 hours
Black-eyed beans	4	1½
Beans, broad and butter beans, scarlet runner beans, split peas	3	1 hour
Split red lentils	2	20 minutes
Soya beans black/white	3	1 hour
Tofu (soya bean curd)	Add to stir frys or casseroles and cook gently for 5-20 minutes.	
Tempeh	Simmer in shoyu water and kombu, to cover, cook for 45 minutes or cook in stew.	

Cooking times for beans suitable for pressure cooking

Chick peas (garbanzos)	3	1 hour
Brown/green lentils	3	20 minutes
Black/red kidney beans	4	40 minutes
Black-eyed beans	3	35 minutes
Pinto beans, broad and butter beans, scarlet runner beans, split peas	3	40 minutes
Soya beans black/white	4	3 hours or more

All beans bigger than aduki beans need soaking. If you soak beans overnight, then cook them in the morning, or put them to soak in the morning to cook in the afternoon. More than six hours soaking is not beneficial.

All beans need to be cooked with a 6" strip of kombu or wakame. It increases the digestibility, and adds minerals. Salt or other seasonings should not be added until ten minutes before the end of cooking time. Adding it at the beginning prevents the beans from softening.

Appendix II
Glossary

Agar-Agar
A white gelatin derived from a species of seaweed. Usually in flake form, it is used to make jellies and aspics.

Amazake
Sweet beverage derived from fermented rice.

Arrowroot
A starch flour processed from the root of a native American plant. It is used as a thickening agent, similar to cornstarch or kuzu.

Bancha Tea
Also called kukicha or three year twig tea. It consists of the stems and leaves from tea bushes that are at least three years old. It comes pre-roasted. It contains no chemical dyes, and aids digestion.

Daikon
A long white radish. Daikon is the Japanese name, and mouli is the European name. Alternatively use turnip.

Fu
Steamed wheat gluten.

Gomasio
A condiment made from roasted, ground sesame seeds and sea salt. For young children use no salt or one part to twenty five parts seeds.

Kantan
A jelly dessert made from fruit and agar agar.

Koji
Grain that has been inoculated with the same type of bacteria that is used in making such fermented foods and drinks as miso, tamari, amasake and sake.

Kuzu
A white starch made from the root of the wild kuzu plant. Used as a thickening agent like arrowroot or cornstarch. Must be dissolved in COLD water, it will then thicken in hot water.

Miso
Brown, amber or white fermented flavouring paste made from soya or other beans, grains and sea salt. Buy unpasteurised so that the live enzymes help aid digestion. Add to soups, stews, sauces and dressings.

Mochi
A rice cake or dumpling made from cooked pounded sweet rice. It is effective in enriching and increasing breast milk. Children love it as it is slightly rich in flavour.

Mouli
See daikon.

Natto
Soya beans which have been cooked and mixed with beneficial enzymes and allowed to ferment for twenty four hours under a controlled temperature.

Natto Miso
A condiment miso which is not actually natto. It is made from soya beans, grain, ginger and kombu, and fermented for a short time. Also called 'Natto Miso Chutney'.

Sake
Rice wine

Sea Salt
Salt obtained from the ocean as opposed to land salt. It is either sun dried or kiln baked. High in trace minerals it contains no chemicals, sugar or iodine.

Seitan
Wheat gluten cooked in shoyu, kombu and water.

Shiitake
A medicinal, dried mushroom imported from Japan.

Shiso
Beefsteak plant leaves that have been pickled and are used to flavour foods such as umeboshi plums. They also provide colour — bright red. Also baked and ground into a condiment.

Shoyu
All-purpose 'soya sauce'. The best varieties are prepared from soya beans, natural salt, and well water, fermented together along with a koji starter and roasted cracked wheat.

Squash
A vegetable like pumpkin such as butternut squash, acorn squash or hokkaido.

Suribachi

A special serrated, glazed clay bowl. Used with a pestle (called a surikoji) for grinding and pureeing food.

Sushi

Rice rolled with vegetables, fish or pickles, wrapped in nori and sliced into rounds.

Sushi Mat

A mat made from strips of bamboo and tied together with string. Used in making sushi, or as a cover for bowls of food.

Tacos

Fried and shaped corn pancakes. Used in Mexican cooking.

Tahine

Ground sesame spread sold in jars. The best is roasted sesame seeds. Be careful of any white tahini, as sometimes the sesame seeds are bleached to make them white.

Tempeh

A cultured soya bean cake. It is made from cooked soya beans, vinegar, water and a special bacteria (Rhizopus Oligosporus), and fermented twenty four hours. It is highly nutritious — being a good high quality protein. It is usually sold frozen.

Tempura

Sliced vegetables, fish or tofu etc. which are dipped into batter and fried until golden brown. A favourite with children.

Teriyaki

A soya sauce seasoning/marinade with additional ingredients to give a sweet and sour flavouring to food.

Tofu

Tofu is a soya bean product — often known as soya bean curd. It is white and cheese like in texture. It is high in protein and vitamin B, and is low in calories and fat. It is quite bland in taste, but when well seasoned and combined with other foods it is delicious. Children usually love it. It can be kept — once opened from it's vacuum pack — in water for four days to one week. Change water daily. If any signs of pink it has gone off.

Umeboshi Plums

They are a salt pickled plum, flavoured with shiso leaves. They are excellent for digestion. They can be used in place of sea salt in cooking.

Umeboshi Paste

As above, but not used medicinally — only used in flavouring sauces or vegetable dishes.

Umeboshi Vinegar

Also called red plum seasoning. Used for seasoning salads.

Yin and Yang

These are two energy forces that are complimentary opposites. Yin energy is expansive upward energy. Yang energy is contractive downward energy. Some food examples are:-

YIN	YANG
Fruit	Salt
Grain sweeteners	Kuzu
Leafy greens	Carrots

Yin foods make you relaxed and help you unwind. Yang foods help you to get things organised and be active. We need to include a variety of both types of food in our diet.

Book list for further reading

The Right Food for Your Kids
Louise Templeton   Pub. Century

Cook Yourself A Favour
Drs. J & R Gibson & Louise Templeton   Pub. Thorsons

Macrobiotic Pregnancy and Care of the Newborn
Mishio & Aveline Kushi   Pub. Japan Publications

Natural Child Care An East West Journal Anthology
                                             Pub. East West Books

The Self Healing Cook Book
Kristina Turner   Pub. Earthtones Press

An Introduction to Macrobiotics
Oliver Cowmeadow   Pub. Thorsons

Cooking with Sea Vegetables
Montse & Peter Bradford   Pub. Thorsons

Macrobiotic Cooking
Michele Cowmeadow   Pub. Cornish Connection

Pregnancies & Births of Macrobiotic Women in the United Kingdom
Edited by Linda Hutchinson Burns   (Linda's address is in the
                                             Address List)

Macrobiotic Family Favourites
Wendy Esko & Aveline Kushi   Pub. Japan Publications

Food: Natures Energy Creates You
Peta Jane Gulliver   Pub. Cornish Connection

Childbirth: An Initiation for Women
Peta Jane Gulliver   Pub. Lifeways Publications

Useful Addresses

Genesis Bookshop
188 Old Street, London EC1V 9FR   Mail Order Service

Clearspring Natural Food Store
186 Old Street, London EC1V 9FR   Mail Order Service

East West Center
188 Old Street, London EC1V 9FR   Cooking Classes

Peta Jane & Neil Gulliver
'Lifeways', 2 Capondale Cottages,   Macrobiotic Dietary
New Lane, Holbrook, Suffolk IP9 2RB   Advice, Shiatsu,
                                                     Cooking Classes,
                                                     Lifeways Publications

Linda Hutchinson Burns
1 Sparrow Road, Totnes, Devon TQ9 5PR   Cooking Classes,
                                                     Macrobiotic Studies,
                                                     Dietary & Lifestyle
                                                     Guidance

Marion Price
10 Netherliegh Close, Hornsey Lane,   Cooking Classes,
London N6 5LL   Dietary Advice,
                                                     Cooking Agency

Krysia & Angus Soutar
1 Bourne End Farm Cottages, Wootton,   Macrobiotic Association,
Bedford MK43 9AP   Cooking Classes

Oliver Cowmeadow
The Coach House, Buckyette Farm,   Dietary Advice, Cornish
Littlehempston, Totnes, Devon TQ9 6ND   Connection Publications

Cecilia Armelin, B.Sc.
45 Malborough Road, Donnybrook,   Dietary Advice,
Dublin 4, Eire   Children's Nutritional
                                                     Counselling

Recipe Index

Savoury Dishes

Aduki Bean Burgers	33
Arame Rolls (Pastry)	10
Baked Beans	44
Bean or Tofu Parcel	23
Beans	67
Buckwheat Pancakes	14
Carrot Salad	12
Celery/Cucumber/Orange/Dulse Salad	27
Chickpeas with Carrot & Cauliflower	36
Deep Fried Carrot Tops	47
Dulse Salad	42
Dumplings	21
Fish Spread	40
Fried Beans & Tacos	26
Garlic Fried Rice	20
Golden Millet Croquettes	47
Grain Milk & Baby Rice	50
Grains	66
Green Rolls	42
Grilled Fish	19
Hijiki & Carrots	18
Humous	41
Lentil Picnic Bake	37
Motchi Burgers	16
Noodles with Carrot & Sweetcorn	36
Nori Tempura	44

Parsnip Chips	12
Parsnip Fritters	15
Quick Water Sauteed Greens	45
Red Dragon Pie	28
Red Sauce	39
Rice	28
Sandwiches	18
Sauteed Mushrooms	47
Savoury Tofu on Rice	34
Seitan	14
Seitan Rolls	17
Smoked Tofu Fries	16
Spaghetti	22
Stew	29
Sushi Rolls	10
Tahini on Toast	48
Tempeh "Fingers"	43
Tempeh Triangles	29
Tofu Carrot Sandwiches	31
Tofu Fingers	29
Tofu with Onions & Corn	42
Yellow Split Pea Stew	29

Sweet Dishes

Aduki Bean Dessert	27
Amazake	66
Blackberry & Apple Pie	13
Cake	21

Carrot Cake	13
Cous Cous	30
Crunchy Dessert	29
Custard	29
French Apple Flan	25
Ginger Bread Queens	19
Ginger Pear Kuzu	40
Grape Jelly	26
Hazelnut Biscuits	32
Jam Tarts	20
Lemon Jelly	45
Lemon Pie	38
Mandarin Jelly	26
Oat & Raisin Cookies	34
Quick Cous Cous Cake	37
Rhubarb Crumble	48
Rich Fruit Cake	22
Seed/Nut Balls	31
Semolina Dessert	16
Steamed Marmalade Pudding	24
St.Clements Pudding	25
Tofu Ice Cream	17

Other Books Published by Cornish Connection

INTRODUCTION TO MACROBIOTICS

Oliver Cowmeadow

A clear and simple introduction to the macrobiotic approach to a natural and healthy way of eating and living. It describes a nutritious and well-balanced diet, with details of which foods to eat and to avoid. It considers the dietary causes of common illnesses, and how a change in diet can be used to prevent sickness. **Paperback, 30 pages, £1.95.**

MACROBIOTIC COOKING

Michele Cowmeadow

This book describes how to prepare delicious, nutritious and well-balanced meals including soups, grains, beans and vegetable dishes, sauces and dressings, pickles, condiments and beverages. There are menu plans for 7 days' meals, and a wealth of information for those preparing wholefood and macrobiotic meals. **Paperback, 64 pages, £3.50.**

MACROBIOTIC DESSERTS

Michele Cowmeadow

Desserts are an essential part of most people's diet. This book contains over 80 tempting and delicious sugar-free recipes, using simple and wholesome ingredients like fruits, nuts, seeds, grains and natural sweeteners. A section on Christmas cooking includes recipes for mince pies, Christmas Cake and Pudding. **Paperback, 58 pages, £2.50.**

YIN & YANG: A Practical Guide to Eating a Balanced & Healthy Diet

Oliver Cowmeadow

With the large number of different diets advocated today, the ancient symbols of yin and yang provide an essential guide to the unique benefits and effects of different foods and how to plan a truly balanced and healthy diet. It includes a chart of foods on a yin yang scale, a balanced diet plan, menu plans and recipes, and the physical, emotional and mental benefits of a balanced diet. **Paperback, 82 pages, £3.95.**

FOOD: Nature's Energy Creates You

Peta Jane Gulliver

The theme of this book is the changing of the seasons, and their effect on us and the energies of food. It shows how to choose seasonal foods, including many wild plants, and to celebrate the traditional Celtic festivals eight times a year. Packed with information, 70 delicious recipes, and many attractive drawings. **Paperback, 98 pages, £4.95.**

These books can be ordered from your local bookshop, or obtained directly from the address below. Please add 10% to your order for post and package. Please enquire for details of wholesale terms.

**Cornish Connection, The Coach House, Buckyette Farm,
Littlehempston, Totnes, Devon TQ9 6ND.
Telephone 080426 593.**